OUT OF THE LAB
EXTREME JOBS IN SCIENCE

ZOOLOGISTS AND ECOLOGISTS

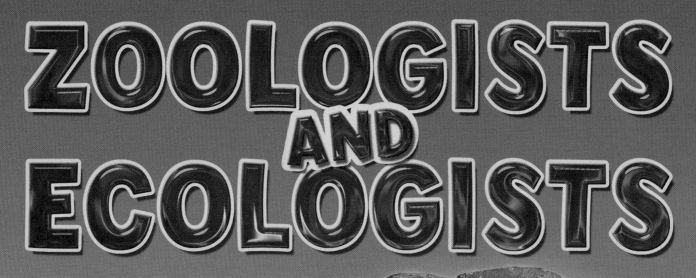

by Ruth Owen

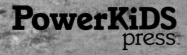

PowerKiDS
press

New York

Published in 2014 by The Rosen Publishing Group, Inc.
29 East 21st Street, New York, NY 10010

First Edition

Produced for Rosen by Ruby Tuesday Books Ltd
Editor for Ruby Tuesday Books Ltd: Mark J. Sachner
US Editor: Joshua Shadowens
Designer: Emma Randall

Photo Credits:
Cover, 1, 5, 7 (bottom), 8–9, 14–15, 18–19, 20–21, 28–29 © Shutterstock; 4 (left) © Frank Vassen; 5 (right) © Roman Klementschitz; 7 (top), 12–13, 16–17, 25, 26–27, © FLPA; 11 © TopFoto; 23 © Jon Brack.

Publisher Cataloging Data

Owen, Ruth.
Zoologists and ecologists / by Ruth Owen. — First edition.
 p. cm. — (Out of the lab: extreme jobs in science)
Includes index.
ISBN 978-1-4777-1293-1 (library binding) — ISBN 978-1-4777-1384-6 (pbk.) — ISBN 978-1-4777-1385-3 (6-pack)
1. Zoologists — Juvenile literature. 2. Zoology — Vocational guidance — Juvenile literature. 3. Ecology — Juvenile literature. 4. Ecologists — Vocational guidance. I. Owen, Ruth, 1967–. II. Title. JNF
590.92
OWEN
QL50.5 O94 2014
590.92—dc23

Manufactured in the United States of America

CPSIA Compliance Information: Batch #S13PK8: For Further Information contact Rosen Publishing, New York, New York at 1-800-237-9932

Contents

HELPING THE FREAKS!

Lucy Cooke is a **zoologist** who is on a mission to show the world that an animal doesn't need a cute face and fluffy fur to be important!

Lucy believes that animals such as pandas and orangutans are grabbing all the limelight, while other, less cute, **endangered** animals are ignored. Even though some people may think an animal **species** is ugly or disgusting, those animals have an important role to play on the planet. An animal may eat other animals and keep their numbers under control or be the **prey** of another species. Some animals even help plants survive by eating their seeds and then spreading them to new growing places in their waste!

Lucy's campaign has taken her out of the lab and across the globe to help the world's most freakish animals.

▲ An aye-aye

Naked mole rats live in ▲ underground burrows in deserts and grasslands in Africa.

Lucy's top 10 weird animals includes wobbly-nosed proboscis monkeys that live in rain forests in Borneo. It also includes the tree-dwelling aye-aye from Madagascar and the nearly hairless naked mole rat.

A proboscis monkey

5

STRANGE TV STARS

Lucy traveled across Africa, Asia, and Australia meeting animals and filming them for a TV show called *Freaks and Creeps*. Her journey took her through rain forests and across deserts.

Many people love monkeys, but there's one monkey species that has fewer fans than its cute relatives. Adult male baboons are powerful, with razor-sharp canine teeth. Their looks and sometimes fierce behavior have made many **cultures** believe they are evil. During the filming of her TV show, Lucy met baboons up close at a rescue center. Many of the animals had been taken from the wild as babies to be sold as pets. Lucy helped release a group of baboons from the rescue center back into the wild.

SCIENCE IN ACTION

Lucy met endangered pangolins while filming her show. These strange-looking anteaters from Africa and Asia are being killed to be used in **Chinese medicines**. Over 40,000 pangolins were killed just in 2011!

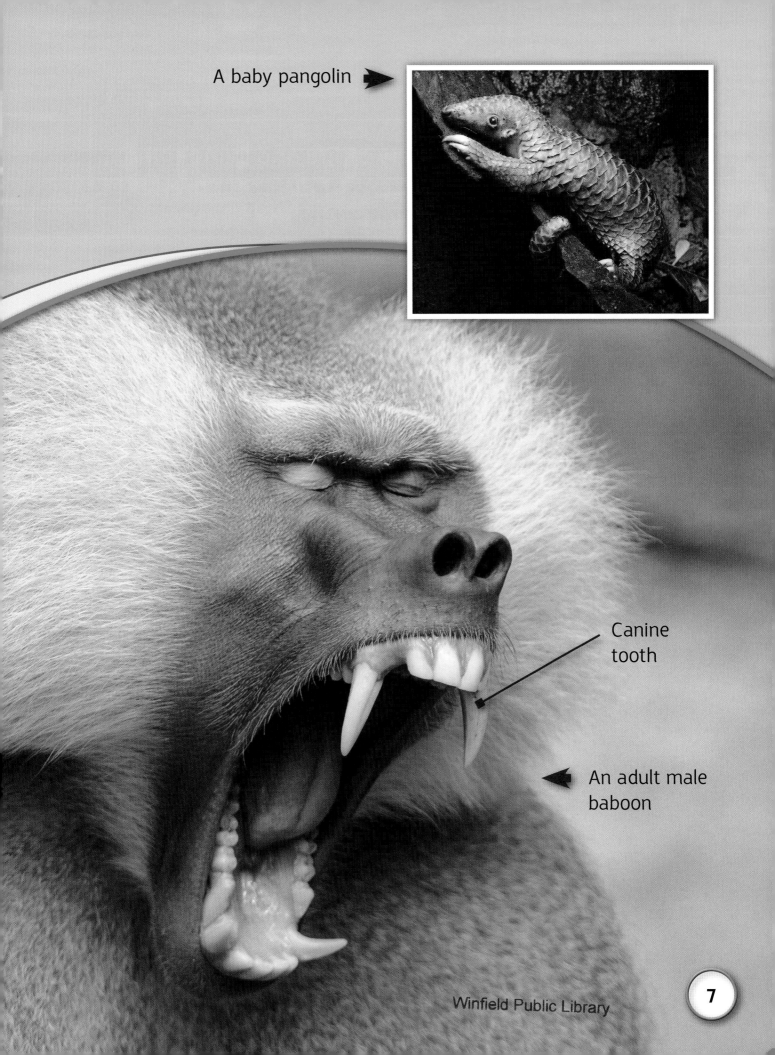

A baby pangolin

Canine tooth

An adult male baboon

WHAT IS A ZOOLOGIST?

Biology is the scientific study of life and living things. This area of science has dozens of different branches. **Zoology** is the branch that relates to the animal kingdom.

Zoologists are scientists who study the physical structure and behavior of animals. They may study living animals and animals that are **extinct.** Zoologists also study the **distribution** of animals across the planet. This means they study where different animal species live. Zoologists are also involved in the scientific **classification** of animals, which is the system for grouping and naming animals. One important reason for classifying animals is to show how they are related to other animals.

SCIENCE IN ACTION

There are different branches within zoology. For example, entomology is the study of insects, while ornithology is the study of birds.

Zoologists get to work up close with wild animals in laboratories, zoos, and in the animals' natural **habitats** such as deserts, grasslands, and rain forests.

This entomologist is studying moths at night.

CRAZY ABOUT CROCODILES

American scientist Brady Barr is a **herpetologist.** Herpetology is the study of **reptiles** and **amphibians.**

One of Brady's biggest achievements was to capture and study all 23 species of crocodiles in the world. It took Brady 15 years to complete his project, and he had to travel to 50 countries.

On another exciting project, Brady teamed up with American **paleontologist** Paul Sereno. Paul had found fossils of an extinct species of giant crocodile in the Sahara Desert. Paul and Brady studied crocodile **fossils** and modern-day live crocodiles. Then they created a life-size reconstruction of the ancient beast. Nicknamed SuperCroc, this prehistoric reptile probably weighed around 20,000 pounds (9,000 kg) and was 40 feet (12 m) long!

Brady Barr (right) with paleontologist Paul Sereno and their model of SuperCroc.

Many crocodile species are critically endangered. The data Brady Barr gathered about the world's 23 different crocodile species will be used to help protect them for the future.

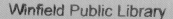

ZOOLOGIST IN DISGUISE

When herpetologist Brady Barr wanted to get up-close with huge Nile crocodiles in Africa, he actually disguised himself as a crocodile!

Brady's disguise comprised a life-like crocodile head made from glass fiber. The head was attached to a long aluminum framework, or cage, the size of an adult Nile crocodile's body.

The cage was covered in Kevlar body armor that looked like tough gray crocodile skin. Hidden inside the cage, Brady then crawled into the middle of a group of crocodiles.

Disguised as a fellow croc, Brady was able to attach small pieces of equipment called data loggers to the crocodiles' tails. The data loggers collected and transmitted information about the crocodiles' lives that scientists could then analyze.

Adult Nile crocodiles can grow to be 20 feet (6 m) long. ▼

SCIENCE IN ACTION

Brady's crocodile costume was plastered in hippopotamus dung to cover up Brady's human smell!

A BIG CAT CAREER

Dr. Alan Rabinowitz is one of the world's leading experts on big cats.

Alan has devoted his zoology career to protecting big cats such as jaguars, snow leopards, and tigers and the wild habitats where they live.

Today, tigers, like many other big cats, are critically endangered. They are hunted by **poachers** and their forest habitat is being destroyed to create farmland and to build towns and roads.

Tigers once lived across Asia, but now there are very few safe places where they can live in the wild. So when Alan heard stories from people living in the foothills of the Himalayas that there was an undiscovered population of tigers high in the mountains, he had to investigate!

While traveling the world studying big cats, Alan has hiked hundreds of miles (km) through thick jungle, caught the dangerous disease malaria, and even survived plane crashes!

◄ Snow leopards are endangered big cats that live in mountains in Asia.

DISCOVERING THE MOUNTAIN TIGERS

Dr. Alan Rabinowitz knew that tigers live in the foothills of the Himalayas in Bhutan, a country in Asia, but could they really survive high in the mountains?

To find out, Alan and a film crew trekked into the mountains. There, they set up camera traps, which are cameras that film anything that causes movement. The camera traps were placed as high as 13,500 feet (4,000 m) up the mountains. At these heights, trees can't even survive to grow.

Three months later, Alan returned to find that the cameras had indeed captured many images of tigers living high in the mountains. Before this discovery, no one knew that tigers could survive in such high places!

This series of tiger photographs were captured using camera traps.

The fact that tigers can survive in mountains is good news. In these remote locations it will be harder for poachers to find them. Also, people cannot build villages or farms on high mountain slopes so the tigers will not compete with humans for space.

NHT 164

NHT 161

NHT 160

NHT 156

COULD YOU BE A ZOOLOGIST?

The best parts about being a zoologist are that your research work or conservation work might help to save an endangered species.

You will get to work with fascinating wild animals and possibly travel the world.

There are downsides, too, though to being a scientist working out of the lab. The places you visit might look beautiful but studying animals such as polar bears or penguins will take you to the coldest places on Earth. In tropical locations you will have to cope with very high temperatures and being bitten by insects as you work.

Also, animals don't stop being animals when 5 pm or the weekend comes around. A zoologist's work can take place day and night, seven days a week!

Whether you work with the same animals every day in a zoo, or study animals in the wild, at some point in your zoology career, you will have to deal with animals you care about dying. This part of a zoologist's work can be very tough!

Studying penguins in Antarctica might seem like a dream job, but could you cope with temperatures many degrees below freezing?

WHAT IS AN ECOLOGIST?

Ecology is the branch of biology that studies the relationships between living things and their **environment.**

Living **organisms** and the nonliving parts of their environment, such as air, water, or soil, form communities known as **ecosystems.** Ecologists study the relationships between the living and nonliving members of an ecosystem.

The organisms studied by ecologists may be as small and simple as the microscopic bacteria that break down dead plants and animals in the soil. They may be as varied as the millions of different types of plants that grow in a rain forest. They may also be as large and complex as elephants, whales, and other **mammals**, including humans.

A scientist uses a zip line to get up close to rain forest treetops.

Ecologists study ecosystems in freezing waters, hot deserts, and many other inhospitable environments. In rain forests, the plants or animals that an ecologist studies may be found 200 feet (61 m) above the ground.

This rope walkway allows people to get close to the tallest trees in a rain forest.

FROM TOILETS TO PLANT FOOD

Haiti is one of the world's poorest countries. When ecologist Sasha Kramer first visited the country in 2004, she realized that most people did not have toilets.

People were dumping their waste in the ocean, in rivers, and around the places they lived. Water and land was becoming polluted, and people were in danger of contracting diseases caused by the **bacteria** in human waste.

Working with an engineer friend, Sasha designed toilets that could be collected from people's homes each week. The waste is then taken to a composting site. Over six months the waste rots down, to become **fertilizer**. The heat produced during this process kills off harmful bacteria. Now, instead of polluting the ground, waste is being used to safely feed the ground and help crops grow.

Sasha Kramer holds a handful of clean, safe fertilizer made from human waste.

Sasha used her understanding of how different living things interact to develop a way to recycle human waste so it could be used to feed plants!

STUDYING CLOUD FORESTS

Greg Goldsmith says life as an ecologist means being a scientist, an explorer, an adventurer, and even a writer.

Greg's research work took him to one of the rarest ecosystems on Earth, the Monteverde cloud forest in Costa Rica. A cloud forest is an evergreen forest situated on the slopes of a mountain. Like a rain forest, this habitat receives lots of rain, but here the clouds actually touch and float among the tops of the trees.

To study the forest, Greg doesn't only spend time on the forest floor. He also works in the canopy, using ropes and mountain-climbing equipment to gain access to the tops of the forest's tall trees.

The Monteverde cloud forest in Costa Rica receives nearly 10 feet (3 m) of rain each year.

In the Monteverde cloud forest, an area just the size of Central Park in New York is home to over 700 different species of trees. In the Monteverde forest there are still new species of plants and animals waiting to be discovered.

LIFE IN THE CLOUD FOREST

In the Monteverde cloud forest there is heavy rainfall for nine months of the year. For the other three months it is completely dry.

Greg Goldsmith wanted to research how the trees and other plants survive these extreme changes in the amount of water they receive. The survival of the forest's trees is important because they provide food and homes for many animals found nowhere else on the planet. As an ecologist, Greg studies how the weather, plants, and animals in the cloud forest interact.

Greg didn't only want other scientists to know about this amazing ecosystem, though. He wanted to find a way for his research to be accessible to people everywhere.

A brown-billed scythebill hummingbird in its tree hole nest in the Monteverde cloud forest

SCIENCE IN ACTION

Greg Goldsmith says that carrying out scientific research is like opening doors. You never know what's going to be on the other side!

OPENING DOORS

Not everyone can explore a cloud forest, so along with two colleagues, photographer Drew Fulton and filmmaker Colin Witherill, Greg Goldsmith has created an amazing online way for people to explore Monteverde.

The *Canopy in the Clouds* project allows students to virtually visit and learn about Monteverde from wherever they are in the world. Using the website, students can watch videos and obtain 360-degree views of the forest as if they were standing on the forest floor and looking in every direction. They can also enjoy viewing the forest from high in the tree canopy.

Like all the scientists in this book, Greg is using his scientific training to help the planet's living things and to help other people learn more about the natural world.

SCIENCE IN ACTION

Before we can protect and help Earth's living things, we need to know what those things are, where they live, and what they need to survive. Zoologists and ecologists are a very important part of that process.

Ecologist Greg Goldsmith has made it possible for students to visit a cloud forest from their classrooms!

GLOSSARY

amphibians (am-FIH-bee-unz) Animals such as frogs, toads, salamanders, and newts. Most amphibians begin their lives in water but live out of water as adults.

bacteria (bak-TIHR-ee-uh) Microscopic living things. Some bacteria are helpful, while others can cause disease.

Chinese medicines (chy-NEEZ MEH-duh-sinz) Traditional medicines that sometimes include the body parts of animals, even though those body parts have no healing powers.

classification (klas-if-ih-KAY-shun) Sorting or arranging things in groups according to their features.

cultures (KUL-churz) Groups of people. The people of a particular culture live and express themselves in the same way through things such as language, dress, food, and celebrations.

distribution (dis-trih-BYOO-shun) Where in the world animals live.

ecologists (ee-KAH-luh-jists) Scientists who specialize in studying living things and their environments.

ecosystems (EE-koh-sis-tuhmz) Communities of living things, such as plants and animals, that share an environment. The nonliving things in an environment, such as water or soil, are also part of the ecosystem.

endangered (in-DAYN-jerd) In danger of no longer existing.

environment (en-VY-ern-ment) The area where plants and animals live, along with all the things, such as weather, that affect the area.

extinct (ik-STINGKT) No longer existing.

fertilizer (FUR-tuh-lyz-er) Chemicals or natural materials, such as waste, used to feed plants.

habitats (HA-buh-tats) Places where an animal or plant species usually lives. A habitat may be a rain forest, the ocean, or a backyard.

herpetologist (her-puh-TAH-leh-jist) A scientist who specializes in studying reptiles and amphibians.

mammals (MA-mulz) Warm-blooded animals that have a backbone and hair, breathe air, and feed milk to their young.

organisms (OR-guh-nih-zumz) Living things.

paleontologist (pay-lee-on-TO-luh-jist) A scientist who studies animals and plants from the past by examining fossils.

poachers (POH-cherz) People who break the law by killing animals or taking them from their natural habitat.

prey (PRAY) An animal that is hunted by another animal as food.

reptiles (REP-tylz) Animals such as snakes, lizards, turtles, crocodiles, and alligators that are cold-blooded and have scaly skin.

species (SPEE-sheez) One type of living thing. The members of a species look alike and can produce young together.

zoologist (zoh-AH-luh-jist) A scientist who specializes in studying animals.

zoology (zoh-AH-luh-jee) The branch of biology that deals with the scientific study of animals.

WEBSITES

Due to the changing nature of Internet links, PowerKids Press has developed an online list of websites related to the subject of this book. This site is updated regularly. Please use this link to access the list:

www.powerkidslinks.com/olejs/zoo/

READ MORE

Latham, Donna. *Ecology*. Sci-Hi: Life Science. Mankato,MN: Raintree, 2009.

Slade, Suzanne. *What Can We Do About Endangered Animals?* Protecting Our Planet. New York: PowerKids Press, 2009.

Wood, Alix. *Weird Animals in the Wild*. Earth's Grossest Animals. New York: Windmill Books, 2013.